Tigwell, Tony
Sakina in India.—(Beans)
1. Takukobowli (Uttar Pradesh, India)—Social life and customs—Juvenile literature
I. Title II. Series
954'.2 DS486.T/

ISBN 0-7136-2243-1

A&C Black (Publishers) Limited
35 Bedford Row, London WC1R 4JH

Acknowledgments
The map is by Tony Garrett

Filmset by August Filmsetting, Warrington, Cheshire.
Printed in Hong Kong by Dai Nippon Printing Co. Ltd.

Sakina in India

Tony Tigwell

Adam & Charles Black · London

My name is Sakina. I am ten years old. I live in a village called Takukibowli, in Northern India. It's near the famous city of Varanasi (sometimes written as Benares) on the river Ganges.

My dad is called Karam Ali and my mum's name is Sabun Nisa Bibi. My brother is called Asharap. He's only six years old but he's very cheeky. We are standing in front of our house. I get shy when anyone takes my picture.

Mum is wearing a cotton *sari*, but I'm wearing my *shalwar* (baggy trousers), *kameez* (tunic) and *dupatta* (scarf). Dad looks serious but he's very kind and likes playing with us.

CHINA
HIMALAYAS
PAKISTAN
NEPAL
UTTAR PRADESH
INDIA
BANGLADESH
SRI LANKA
HIMALAYAS
NEPAL
SIKKIM
BHUTAN
Kathmandu
River Ganges
Varanasi
Takukibowli
Sakina lives here
BANGLADESH
N
Calcutta
150miles
150km

We speak Hindi and I'm learning to write Hindi at school. I dip a bamboo pen into white ink made with chalk and write words on a black wooden slate. It's easy to wash the letters off and start again.

Asharap and I walk to school at about eight o'clock in the morning, after our breakfast of wheat porridge and sugar cane juice. My friend Shushma comes from her house to meet us. She's picked some fresh chick-peas for us to eat on the way to school.

Although Asharap is four years younger than me, I am only one year ahead of him at school. This is because my parents often keep me at home to help in the house.

At school, our teacher is very strict. She makes us sit in straight lines. We learn arithmetic and the history and geography of India. We come home at midday. In the afternoons, the teacher has a different class.

Our house is at one end of the village, beside the main road. The centre of the village is a busy place. People from the nearby villages often come to Takukibowli to do their shopping. There are shops selling tea, salt, oil, batteries, cloth and all sorts of other things. One man sells biscuits, peanuts and salty snacks from his hand cart.

No one in our village has a car. Many of the men have bicycles – you can see my dad's bicycle leaning against the wall of the house. It's made in India and its trade mark is 'Hero'. Indian bicycles are very strong because the roads are so uneven.

In winter, when the sun is not too hot, we like to sit out in front of our house and watch people going along the road.

Sometimes, the express bus to Allahabad goes past. When it passes our house, we get covered in dust. In the monsoon season, when it rains a lot, we get splattered with mud. It will be much better when the road is repaired and has a layer of tarmac.

My dad built our house with the help of neighbours. It is made of bricks and plastered with clay. The bricks are made at a kiln down the road. The young girls who work at the kiln carry heavy loads on their heads. They don't get paid much for such hard work. The tiles on our roof are made by a local potter.

We are a Muslim family. When anyone comes to see us, we say 'Asalaam alaicum' which means 'God bless you'. We are the only Muslim family in Takukibowli, all our neighbours are Hindu.

This is one of our neighbours. Her name is Balukhnibai. She's always saying funny things to make us laugh. She is going to dig in the fields, with her husband. The earth is very hard, so she carries a *powra* to dig with. It has a blade and is used like a pick.

Balukhnibai's husband is ploughing one of the fields near his house. He uses the stick to prod the bullocks when they stop. After he's ploughed the field, he will plant chick-peas.

Most of the families in our village are farmers. They grow wheat, sugar cane, lentils and vegetables.

My parents both work at home. My dad is a weaver. There are two looms in the front room of our house. They are set into pits in the clay floor. Dad sits on a plank with his feet on the pedals. He and his friend, Balikaran, begin work as soon as it is light. We are woken up by the 'clack-clack' sound of the looms.

Dad and Balikaran weave borders which are cut up and sewn onto saris. Dad sells the borders for eight rupees a metre. He can weave about six metres a day. We can buy a bar of soap for one rupee, or an aluminium cooking pot for eight rupees.

The silver thread which dad uses is expensive, so he works carefully. The shuttle which weaves in and out of the threads is made of polished buffalo horn. It has to be smooth, or it might tear the fine threads.

Lots of wire and string lead from each loom to a box above it. Balikaran is fixing a set of cards into the box above his loom. The cards have holes punched in them. Each set of cards will adjust the loom to weave a different pattern.

The wooden frame for the loom was made by the carpenter in Takukibowli. Here, he's using an adze to shape part of a new frame for a loom.

My dad was trained as a weaver at Sevapuri Ashram, about three kilometres from our village.

This is Mr Iqbal Singh, standing outside a workshop at the Ashram. He and his friends also train local people to make tiles, soap, matches and other useful things. They are followers of a great man called Mahatma Gandhi.

There's also a clinic at the Ashram, where we can go when we are ill.

My mum hel
thread from
into the shut
wheel is mad
she can close
In the evenin
Mum also se
Glass bangl

At the back of our house, there are two rooms. One is a storeroom where we keep spare parts for the looms. The other is the kitchen and bedroom. Asharap and I are sitting on the rope netting of our bed. It is called a *charpoy*. Our parents have one, too. The beds are light and easy to carry. In summer, we take them outside and sleep under the stars. But in winter, we're glad to snuggle up under our cotton quilts.

Mum is winnowing wheat. She flicks the basket up and down. All the unwanted stones and pieces of straw are separated from the wheat and knocked out of the basket. When the wheat has been winnowed, mum will grind it into flour. Then she can make *chapattis*, a kind of flat round bread.

The fireplace is in one corner of the room, near the back door. Mum made the fireplace herself, with clay. We burn a mixture of wood and dry cow dung. There aren't many trees where we live and wood is expensive. Our house doesn't have a chimney, so the smoke drifts out through gaps between the roof tiles. We eat mutton or vegetables and lentils with *chapattis* or rice.

Dad buys the rice and lentils at the shops, but a lady comes to the house selling vegetables. Today, she has some spinach. Can you see what she is using as a weight on her scales?

We keep one chicken and a goat, so we can have fresh eggs and goat's milk. Asharap looks after the chicken. That's an easy job. The goat is always giving me trouble. She bites through her rope and runs off to eat the farmers' crops. I've put a brass bell around her neck so that I can hear where she is.

I cut grass from the banks around the sides of the fields and carry it home in a basket for the goat to eat. When the fields are wet, I wear my plastic sandals.

Another of my jobs is to fetch water from the well. We share the well with ten other families. Everyone is careful to keep the well clean, so we can have fresh water to drink. Although the well is deep, the water level becomes low in the dry months of the year. We make sure that none of the water is wasted and we look forward to the first monsoon rains, in June, when the well will fill up again.

Sometimes, I help mum to wash our clothes. I rub them with a bar of hard soap. Then I bash them on the stone slab. I didn't crack the stone though!

When it's sunny, I lay the clothes out on the ground to dry. But if it rains, I hang them on a line inside the house.

Across the fields at the back of the house lives a rich farmer. He has a modern well with a pump to irrigate his land. Sometimes we go over to his farm to wash our clothes and have a bath. On a hot day, it's very refreshing because the cool water comes from deep down in the ground.

When dad has finished weaving, he wants to relax. He lights his *hookah* and has a quiet smoke. The *hookah* makes a bubbling noise as he draws the smoke through water in the coconut bowl of the pipe. The tobacco in the clay top is kept alight with burning charcoal. It's winter, so dad is wearing a woollen jumper. The blue cotton garment is called a *lungi*.

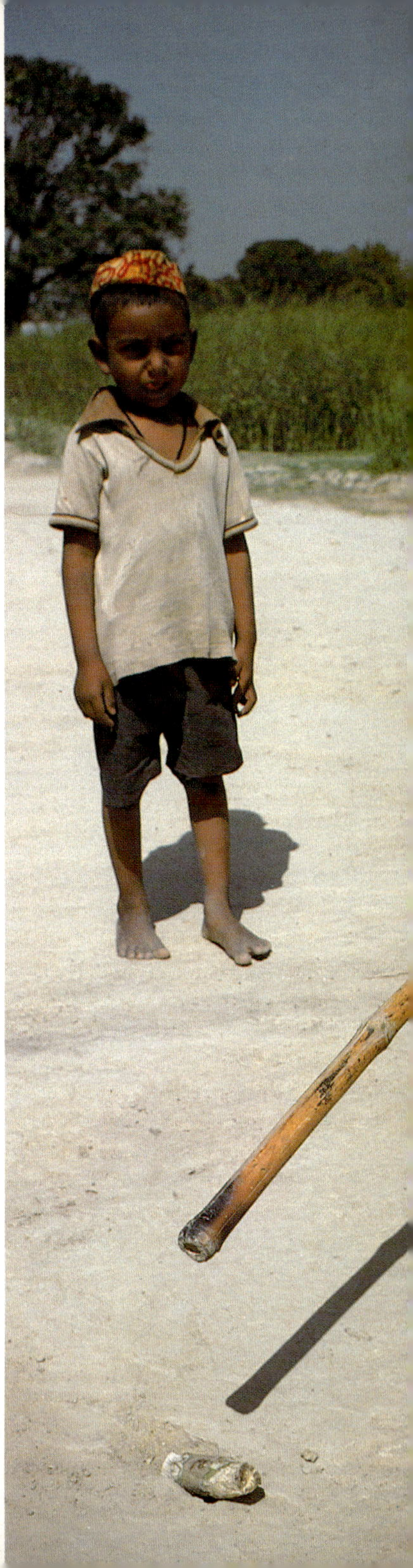

We don't have a radio or a television. In the evenings, we sing songs and listen to stories. Sometimes, we play a game called *guli danda*. We take it in turns to hit a small wooden peg with a stick. When the peg spins in the air, we try to hit it again and send it as far as we can.

Asharap is playing a game called *pithoo*. It's a team game. He throws the ball to knock over a pile of seven pieces of broken roof tile. Then, his team have to pile them up again before the others can hit them with the ball.

Every Friday, my dad cycles to the mosque to pray. It has been built at a crossroads. Muslims come from all the surrounding villages to meet at the mosque. On his way home, dad may buy some mutton from a Muslim butcher who has set up his stall at the crossroads.

We have a calendar on the wall in our house. It shows a boy reading our holy book, the Koran. We bought it from a man who sells them on the pavement in Varanasi. Can you pick out the Muslim calendars in his display?

Once a month, dad travels into Varanasi to sell his *sari* borders to merchants and to buy more thread. We look forward to the times when he takes us with him. We walk along paths through the fields to Sevapuri station. There is always time for a cup of tea while we wait for the train. The cups are made of clay and we throw them away when we've drunk the tea.

The passenger train is slow. It takes an hour to reach Varanasi, because the train stops at every station.

In the big city, we stick close together. I'm always afraid of getting lost in the busy streets and bazaars. There's so much to see. It's very noisy, too, with the shouts of traders and the ringing of bicycle bells. The best way to travel is in a tricycle rickshaw or in a horse-drawn tonga. When we've finished our shopping, we take a tricycle rickshaw back to the station.

Varanasi is a famous city. Hindu pilgrims come from all over India to bathe in the river Ganges. It's a holy river for Hindus. There are temples all along the river bank. Foreign tourists go out in boats to take photographs of the scenery.

We leave Varanasi as the sun sets. Each of us has something to show the neighbours – a bright aluminium cooking pot for mum, a toy snake for Asharap, a new *lungi* for dad and a pair of plastic sandals for me. As the passenger train clicks across the iron bridge over the river, Asharap and I fall asleep.